Korean Children's Favorite Folk Tales

Edited by Peter Hyun
Illustrated by Dong-il Park

HOLLYM
Elizabeth, NJ · SEOUL

Korean Children's Favorite Folk Tales

Copyright © 1978, 1995
by Korean Overseas Information Service

First published in 1978
by Saem Toh Publishing Co.
1-115, Tongsung-dong, Chongno-gu, Seoul, Korea
Under the title of "It's Fun Being Young In Korea"

Second revised edition, 1995
Second printing, 2000
Published by Hollym International Corp.
18 Donald Place, Elizabeth, New Jersey 07208, U.S.A.
Tel:(908)353-1655 Fax:(908)353-0255
http://www.hollym.com

Published simultaneously in Korea
by Hollym Corporation; Publishers
13-13 Kwanchol-dong, Chongno-gu, Seoul 110-111, Korea
Tel:(02)735-7551～4 Fax:(02)730-5149, 8192
http://www.hollym.co.kr

ISBN: 1-56591-064-8

Printed by Korea

Contents

Preface

This book is dedicated to the children of the world in commemoration of the International Year of the Child 1979.

Its purpose is to present a glimpse of the fantasies that occupied the minds and hearts of Korean children during the struggling years when the nation was known as the Hermit Kingdom, and, with the inclusion of three modern short stories, a brief picture of what the children of later generations were learning.

Although incomplete in that it does not contain every folktale of the land that has been preserved through the centuries, it is felt the ones gathered here are the most representative of this area of Korea's folklore and will offer the fairest cross-section.

It is hoped that through the publication and dissemination of books such as this the children of the world will learn that they are all very much alike.

Grateful acknowledgement is extended to:

Frances Carpenter Huntington who allowed use of *The Dog and the Cat* and *The Ant That Laughed Too Much* from her *Tales of a Korean Grandmother;*

Zong In-sob for the use of *The Heavenly Maiden and the Woodcutter* and *The Three Sons* from his *Folk Tales from Korea;*

Ha Tae-hung for the use of *The Hare's Liver* from his *Folk Tales of Old Korea;*

the late Pyun Yong-tae who translated *Kongji and Patji.*

Korean Children's Favorite Folk Tales

The Heavenly Maiden and the Woodcutter

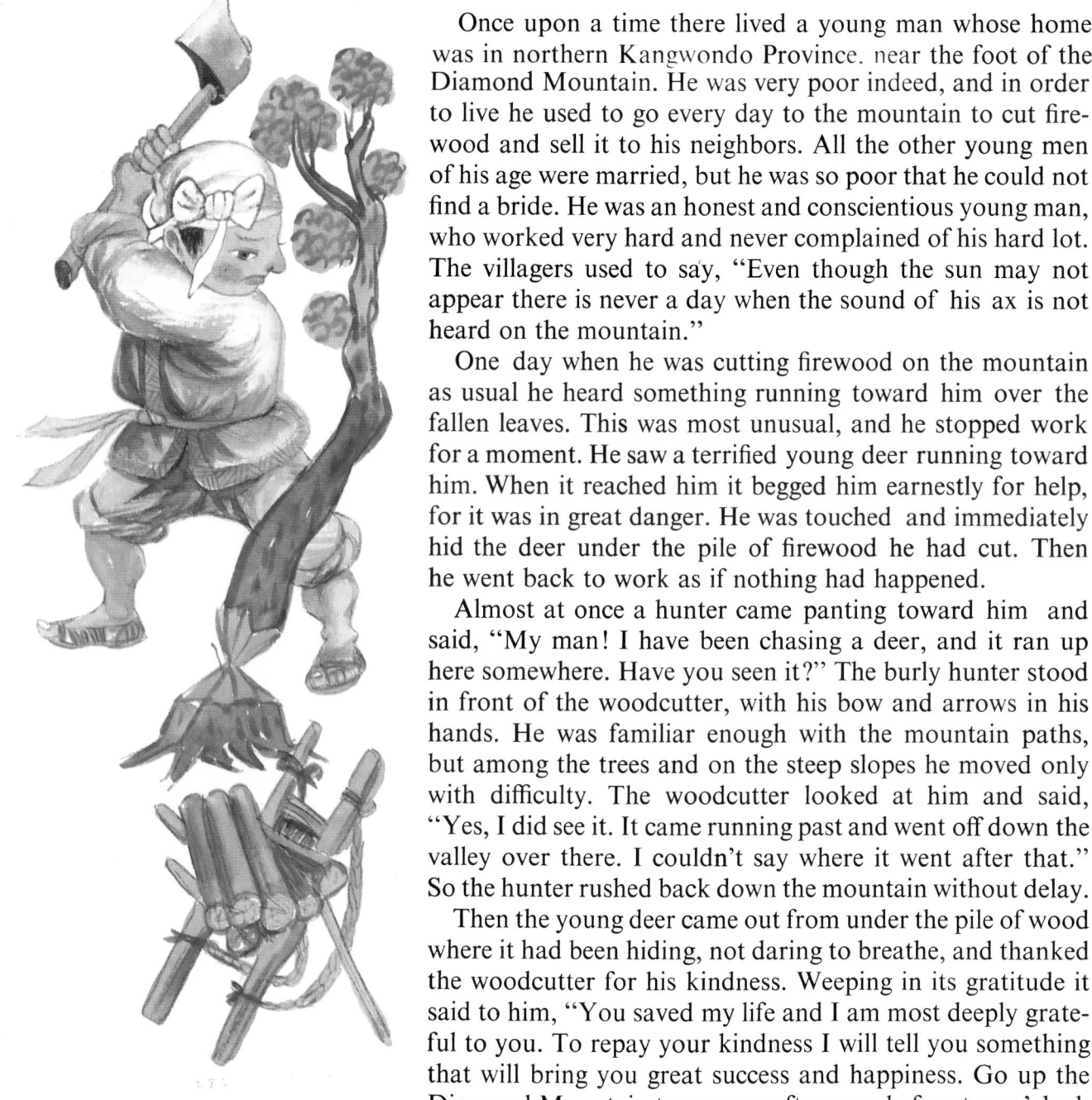

Once upon a time there lived a young man whose home was in northern Kangwondo Province, near the foot of the Diamond Mountain. He was very poor indeed, and in order to live he used to go every day to the mountain to cut firewood and sell it to his neighbors. All the other young men of his age were married, but he was so poor that he could not find a bride. He was an honest and conscientious young man, who worked very hard and never complained of his hard lot. The villagers used to say, "Even though the sun may not appear there is never a day when the sound of his ax is not heard on the mountain."

One day when he was cutting firewood on the mountain as usual he heard something running toward him over the fallen leaves. This was most unusual, and he stopped work for a moment. He saw a terrified young deer running toward him. When it reached him it begged him earnestly for help, for it was in great danger. He was touched and immediately hid the deer under the pile of firewood he had cut. Then he went back to work as if nothing had happened.

Almost at once a hunter came panting toward him and said, "My man! I have been chasing a deer, and it ran up here somewhere. Have you seen it?" The burly hunter stood in front of the woodcutter, with his bow and arrows in his hands. He was familiar enough with the mountain paths, but among the trees and on the steep slopes he moved only with difficulty. The woodcutter looked at him and said, "Yes, I did see it. It came running past and went off down the valley over there. I couldn't say where it went after that." So the hunter rushed back down the mountain without delay.

Then the young deer came out from under the pile of wood where it had been hiding, not daring to breathe, and thanked the woodcutter for his kindness. Weeping in its gratitude it said to him, "You saved my life and I am most deeply grateful to you. To repay your kindness I will tell you something that will bring you great success and happiness. Go up the Diamond Mountain tomorrow afternoon before two o'clock and when you come to the lakes that lie between the peaks at the foot of the rainbow conceal yourself among the bushes by the water's edge. Then you will see eight Heavenly Maidens come down from the corner of Heaven to bathe in the lakes. While they are bathing they will hang their silken robes on the pine trees by the shore. Do not let them see you, but go secretly and hide one of these garments. Then when they finish bathing one of them will not be able to return to Heaven. Go to her and welcome her, and she will go with you. You will live happily with her, and children will be born

to you, but you must not return her robes to her until you have four children." With these words the deer vanished, leaving the young man overjoyed at what he had heard.

The next morning the young man got up very early and climbed to the peaks of the Diamond Mountain where there

were eight beautiful lakes. The mountain is so beautiful that there is an old proverb which says, 'Do not speak of scenic beauty until you have seen the Diamond Mountain.' It is a spot far from the bustle of everyday life and has been held sacred from the earliest times, so that great temples have been built there. Precipitous peaks soar into the blue sky and trees that have been growing for untold centuries form dense forests where the light of day scarcely penetrates. Streams as clear as crystal flow among the rocks in the valleys, and here and there are lakes and waterfalls, melodious with the songs of birds and the cries of animals.

The young man concealed himself among the bushes and waited. Suddenly, in a corner of the sky, the clouds began to move, and eight Heavenly Maidens came floating down to the lakes at the rainbow's end. They chattered merrily to one another, and all at once took off their robes and hung them on the pine trees. Then each leapt into the clear water of one of the eight lakes. As they swam in the water the woodcutter gazed spellbound. After a while he came to his senses and recalled the advice that the deer had given him. He crept stealthily to the pine trees where they had hung their robes and took those belonging to the youngest Maiden.

Toward sunset the Heavenly Maidens prepared to return

to Heaven. They began to put on their robes but, to the astonishment of all, the youngest Maiden could not find hers. The others could not wait for her, so they climbed up the rainbow to the sky and left her behind. She stood there utterly bewildered, wondering where to find her clothes, when she suddenly saw the young woodcutter standing before her. It was nearly dark, and the young man apologized profusely for the trouble he had caused her and begged her to forgive him. He was very kind and attentive to her, and he took her to his home.

At first the Heavenly Maiden found the customs of life on earth most confusing, but she soon settled down happily to the routine of domestic life. The months passed happily by, and then she gave birth to a son. Her young husband was overjoyed and loved her with all his heart, and his mother too rejoiced in their happiness.

The Heavenly wife seemed utterly contented and lived in harmony with her family. When their second child was born they were happier than ever.

One day the wife asked her husband to return her Heavenly robes. "I have borne you two children. Can't you trust me now?" But her husband refused, for he was afraid that she might carry his children off, one in each arm.

When their third child was born she implored him earnestly again to return her garments. She served him delicious food and wine, trying to allay his supicions. "My dearest husband! I have three children now. Please just let me see my robes. I can hardly betray you now, can I?"

The young man was sympathetic to his wife's feelings and now showed her the garments which he had kept hidden so long.

But alas! When she put them on again she regained her magic powers and at once went up to the sky, holding one child between her legs and one in each arm.

Her husband was stricken with grief and reproached himself for not having followed the deer's advice to the end. He went out to the mountain to cut firewood, and sat at the same place where he had seen the deer before, hoping that it might reappear. By good fortune it passed that way, and he told it his sad story. The deer said to him, "Since the day you hid the Heavenly Maiden's robes, they do not come down to bathe there any more. So if you wish to find your wife and children you must go to them yourself. Happily, there is a way. Go to the same lake tomorrow, and wait until you see a bucket come down on a rope from Heaven. They drop it to fetch up water from the lake for bathing. You must seize

it and empty the water out quickly. Then get in it yourself. They will pull it up at once, for they will not realize that you are in it. That is the only way you will be able to see your family in Heaven." When it had told him this the deer disappeared.

The woodcutter took its advice and was able to go up to Heaven. When he arrived there the Heavenly Maidens said, "This smells like a man!" and, finding him in the bucket, asked him why he had come. He told them, and they took him before the Heavenly King. There he met his wife and children, for she was the daughter of the Heavenly King.

The King allowed him to stay, and he lived very happily in the Heavenly Kingdom. He had the most delicious food to eat every day, and the most beautiful clothes to wear, and there was nothing at all to worry him.

One day, however, he thought regretfully of his mother whom he had left alone on earth, and told his wife that he would like to go and visit her once again. But his wife begged him not to go, for if he once met his mother he would not be able to come back to Heaven again. But he persisted in his request and promised he would come back without fail. So in the end she yielded to his entreaties and said, "I will

get a dragonhorse for you. You will ride on it and it will take you down to earth in the twinkling of an eye. But whatever you do, do not dismount from it, for if your feet once touch the ground you can never come back to me."

The woodcutter mounted the dragonhorse and went down to his mother's house. His mother was overjoyed to see her son again after his long absence. They chatted happily together, and when he bade her farewell, still astride the dragonhorse, his mother said, "I have cooked some pumpkin porridge for you. Please have just one bowl." He could not disappoint her and took the bowl she offered him. But the bowl was so hot that he dropped it on the horse's back. The horse reared violently throwing him to the ground. Neighing loudly the dragonhorse flew up into the sky and disappeared.

So the woodcutter never went back to Heaven and used to stand every day in tears looking up at the sky. At last he died of his grief and was transformed into a cock. So tradition says that the reason why cocks climb to the highest part of the roof and crow with their necks stretched out toward Heaven is that the woodcutter's spirit has entered them and seeks the highest place it can find.

The Dog and the Cat

One warm autumn afternoon sounds of barking from the outer court drifted to the veranda where Ok Cha was helping her grandmother sort pine seeds for New Year cakes.

"I have a riddle for you, Grandma," the little girl said.

"My ears are open, child," the old woman replied, smiling fondly down upon her favorite granddaughter.

"Here it is then: Who in this house first goes forth to welcome the arriving guest?"

"Would it be your father, the master of our house?" the grandmother asked thoughtfully, pretending she had never heard this old riddle before.

"No, Grandma, it would not be Dad. The master of the house greets his guests only when they have entered the outer court." Ok Cha was delighted because her grandmother did not guess the answer at once.

"Would it be Pak, the gatekeeper?" Grandma asked, wrinkling her smooth, old, ivory-colored brow, as if she were puzzled.

"Oh no, Grandma. Shall I tell you? It's Dog!"

"To be sure it is Dog," said the grandmother nodding her dark head, "Dog is the true gatekeeper of our house."

Most of the day, and even at night, this shaggy shepherd, which everyone inside the Kim courts simply called "Dog," lay halfway through the opening cut in the bottom of the bamboo gate. With his head thrust through the opening, he was the first to see and give warning of approaching visitors.

Dog took his duties as gatekeeper much more seriously than the real gatekeeper, who slept most of the time in the door of the servants' houses just inside the gate.

Of course, Dog now and then went out into the street to hunt bits of food that might have been thrown out there by the neighbors. Or he sometimes left his post to bark at a bird or to chase a stray cat.

As a matter of fact it was this last pastime that brought Dog now racing through the middle gate and into the inner court. Around the tall pottery water jars went the black cat with the brown dog at her tail. Over and under the seesaw they flew, and into the corner where Ok Cha's brother, Yong Tu, and his cousins were busy making kites they were going to fly on New Year's.

"Stop, Dog! Come here," Yong Tu called severely. And the boy joined in the chase, finally catching the excited dog by the neck and holding him tight until the black cat got away to safety in the garden beyond the houses.

The children did not have much sympathy for the cat,

but Yong Tu was afraid the animals might spoil his precious kite-making materials which were spread out on the ground. The Kims liked Dog because he was such a good watchman. But he was in no way an indoor pet like the dogs of Western lands. The black cat, which often crept over their wall, was

very wild. Once, Ok Cha had tried to pet it, but the cat would only growl, spit at her, and scratch.

"Why do dogs and cats fight so, Grandma?" the little girl asked, looking up from her tray of pine seeds.

"My grandmother used to tell me a story about that," the old woman said, "and I'll tell it to you." Somehow, Yong Tu and his cousins must have guessed their grandmother was beginning a story. Before she was well started, they had brought their paper, their bamboo sticks, and their gluepots and set up their little kite factory at her feet.

"The dog and the cat in my tale lived in a small wineshop on the bank of a broad river beside a ferry. Old Koo, the shopkeeper, had neither wife nor child. In his little hut he lived by himself except for this dog and cat. They never left his side. While he sold wine in the shop, the dog kept guard at the door and the cat caught mice in the storeroom. When he walked on the river bank, they trotted by his side. When he lay down to sleep, they crept close to his side. They were good enough friends then, the dog and the cat, but that was before the disaster occurred and the cat behaved so badly.

"Old Koo was poor, but he was honest and kind. His shop was not like those where travelers are persuaded to drink wine until they become drunk and roll on the ground. Only one kind of wine was sold, but it was a good wine. Once they had tasted it, Koo's customers came back again and again to fill their long-necked wine bottles.

" 'Where does Old Koo get so much wine?' the neighbors used to ask one another. 'No new jars are ever delivered by ox carts to his door. He makes no wine himself, yet his black jug is never without wine to pour for his customers.'

"No one knew the answer to the riddle save Old Koo himself, and he told it to no one except his dog and cat. Years before he opened his wineshop, Koo had worked on the ferry. One cold rainy night when the last ferry had returned, a strange traveler came to the gate of his hut.

" 'Honorable Sir,' he begged Koo. 'Give me a drop of good wine to drive out the damp chill.'

" 'My wine jug is almost empty,' Koo told the traveler. 'I have only a little for my evening drink, but no doubt you need the wine far more than I. I'll share it with you.' And he filled up a bowl for his strange, thirsty guest.

"The stranger, upon leaving, put into the ferryman's hand a bit of bright golden amber. 'Keep this in your wine jug,' he said, 'and it will always be full.'

"Now, as Old Koo told his dog and cat, that traveler must have been a spirit from Heaven, for when Koo lifted the black jug, it was heavy with wine. When he filled his bowl from it, he thought he had never tasted a drink so sweet and so rich. No matter how much he poured, the wine in the jug never grew less.

"Here was a treasure indeed. With a jug that never ran dry, he could open a wineshop. He would no longer have to go back and forth, back and forth, in the ferryboat over the river in all kinds of weather.

"All went well until one day when he was serving a traveler, Koo found to his horror that his black jug was empty. He shook it and shook it, but no answering tinkle came from the hard amber charm that should have been inside.

" 'Oh My! Oh My!' Koo wailed. 'I must unknowingly have poured the amber out into the bottle of one of my customers. Oh My! What shall I do?'

"The dog and the cat shared their master's sadness. The dog howled at the moon, and the cat prowled around the shop, sniffing and sniffing under the rice jars and even high up on the rafters.

" 'I am sure I could find the charm,' the cat said to the

dog, 'if I could only catch its amber smell.'

" 'We shall search for it together,' the dog said. 'We shall go through every house in the neighborhood. When you sniff it out, I will run home with it.'

"So they began their quest. They asked all the cats and dogs they met for news of the lost amber. They prowled about all the houses, but not a trace could they find of their master's magic charm.

" 'We must try the other side of the river,' the dog said at last. 'They will not let us ride across on the ferryboat. But when the winter cold comes and the river's stomach is solid, we can safely creep over the ice, like everyone else.'

"Thus it was that one winter morning the dog and the cat crossed the river to the opposite side. As soon as the owners were not looking, they crept into the houses. The dog sniffed round the courtyards, and the cat climbed up on the beams under the sloping grass roofs. Day after day, week after week, month after month, they searched and they searched, but with no success.

"Spring was at hand. The joyful fish in the river were

bumping their backs against the soft ice. At last, one day, high up on the top of a great brassbound chest, the cat smelled the amber. But, alas! The welcomed scent came from inside a tightly closed box. What could they do? If they pushed the box off the chest and let it break on the floor, the master of the house would surely be warned and chase them away.

" 'We must get help from the rats,' the clever dog cried. 'They can gnaw a hole in the box for us and get the amber out. In return, we can promise to let them live in peace for ten years.' This was against the nature of any cat, but this one loved its master and consented.

"The rats consented, too. It seemed to them almost too good to be true that both the cats and the dogs might leave them alone for ten whole peaceful years.

"It took the rats many days to gnaw a hole in the box, but at last it was done. The cat tried to get at the amber with its soft paw, but the hole was too small. Finally, a young mouse had to be sent in through the wee hole. It succeeded

in pulling the amber out with its teeth.

" 'How pleased our master will be! Now good luck will live again under his roof,' the cat and the dog said to each other. In their joy at finding the lost amber charm, they ran round and round as if they were having fits.

" 'But how shall we get the amber back to the other side of the river?' the cat cried in dismay. 'You know I cannot swim.'

" 'You shall hold the amber safely inside your mouth, cat,' the dog replied wisely. 'You shall climb on my back, and I'll carry you across the river.'

"And so it happened. Clawing the thick shaggy hair of the dog's back, that cat kept its balance until they had almost reached their own bank of the stream. But there, playing along the shore, were a number of children, who burst into laughter when they saw the strange ferryman and his curious passenger. A cat riding on the back of a dog! 'Ho! Ho! Ho!' they laughed. 'Ha! Ha! Ha! Ho! Ho! Ho! Just look at that.' They called to their parents, and they came to laugh, too.

"Now the faithful dog paid no attention to their foolish mirth, but the cat could not help joining them in the fun. It, too, began to laugh, and from its open mouth Old Koo's precious amber charm dropped into the river.

"The dog shook the cat off his back, he was so angry, and it was a miracle that the cat at last got safely to the shore. In a rage the dog chased the cat, which finally took refuge up a tree. There the cat shook the moisture out of its fur. By spitting and spitting, it got rid of the water it had swallowed while in the river. The cat dared not come down out of the tree until the angry dog had gone away.

"That, so my grandmother said, is why the dog and the cat are never friends, my dear ones. That is why, too, a cat always spits when a strange dog comes too near. That is also why a cat does not like to get its feet wet."

"But what about the amber charm and poor Old Koo?" Ok Cha asked anxiously.

"It was the dog who finally saved the fortunes of the old wineshop keeper," the old woman explained. "First, he tried swimming out into the stream to look for the amber. But it was too deep for him to see the bottom. Then he sat beside the river fishermen, wishing he had a line or a net like theirs that would bring up the golden prize he sought. Suddenly, from a fish that had just been pulled out of the water, the dog sniffed the amber perfume. Grabbing the fish up in his mouth before the fisherman could stop him, he galloped off home.

" 'Well done, Dog,' said Old Koo. 'There is only a little food left under our roof. This fish will make a good meal for you and me.' The old man cut open the fish and, to his surprise and delight, the amber rolled out.

" 'Now I can put my magic charm back into the jug,' Koo said to himself. 'But there must be at least a little wine in it to start the jug flowing again. While I go out to buy some, I'll just lock the amber up inside my clothes chest.'

"When Koo came back with the wine and opened the chest, he found that instead of the one suit he had stored in it, there were now two. Where his last pouch of cash had been, there were two pouches. And he guessed that the secret of this amber charm was that it would double whatever it touched.

"With this knowledge Koo became rich beyond his wildest dreams. And in the gate of his fine new house he installed a private door for his faithful friend who had saved him from starving. There, day and night, like our four-footed gate guard, the dog lay watching in peace and well-fed contentment. But all through his life he never again killed a mouse nor made a friend of a cat."

The Three Sons

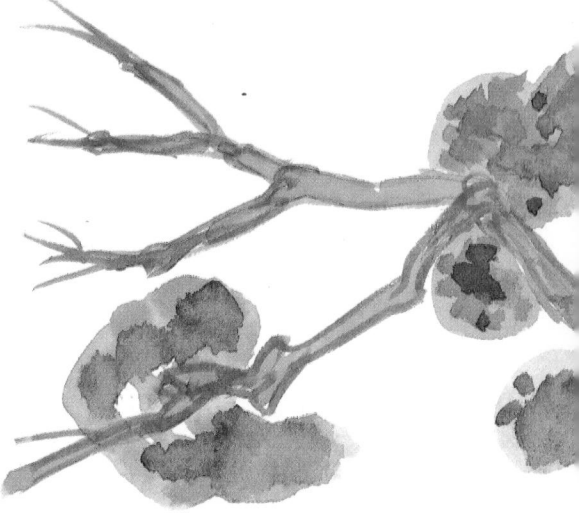

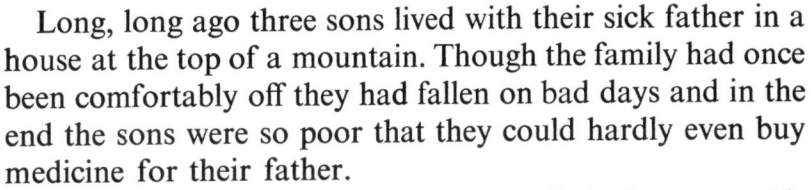

Long, long ago three sons lived with their sick father in a house at the top of a mountain. Though the family had once been comfortably off they had fallen on bad days and in the end the sons were so poor that they could hardly even buy medicine for their father.

At last the old man lay dying. He called his sons to his bedside and bade them farewell with tears in his eyes. "You have toiled hard for me these many years," he said. "While your mother was alive I was rich and had much property. But now I have nothing left but the few things that I will give you as tokens to remember me by. To my eldest son I leave my hand-mill with its grinding stones. To the second I leave my bamboo stick and a bowl made of half a gourd. And to the third I leave my long drum with the narrow waist. May Heaven's blessing light upon you!" With these words he breathed his last.

After the funeral the three brothers agreed to leave the house. They set out carrying the gifts their father had left them, and before long they came to a fork in the mountains where three paths branched out. They agreed to meet again after ten years at that spot, and then they parted, each taking a separate path. The eldest son took the right hand path, the second son the middle, and the youngest the path to the left.

Carrying the heavy millstones on his back, the eldest son walked on until night fell. At last he felt that he could walk no further and lay down under a big tree by the roadside to pass the night. It was a pitch-black night, and he began to feel afraid. He feared that some wild animal or a robber might come and attack him if he stayed there, so he climbed up the tree still carrying the millstones.

In the middle of the night, as he sat drowsily in the tree, he heard men quarrelling on the ground beneath him. He listened and soon realized that they were robbers arguing

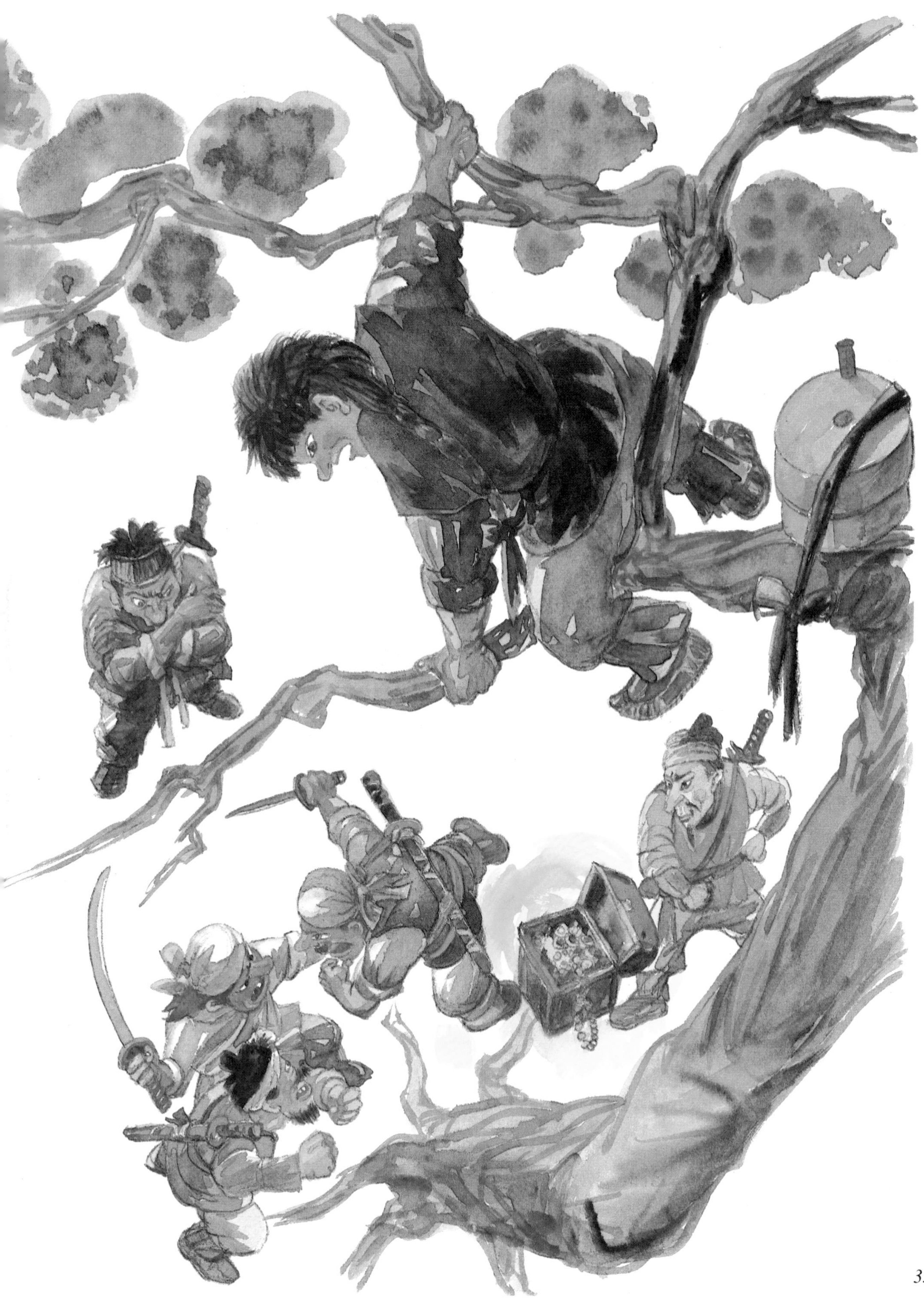

over the division of their loot. He heard the clink of coins being counted.

He began to shake the branches of the tree causing the dew on the leaves to fall off, and at the same time he rubbed his two millstones together so that they made a noise like thunder. Frightened by the thunder and rain the robbers ran away, still shouting abuses at one another. "The punishment of Heaven has fallen upon you, you scoundrel," said one. "It has fallen fair and square on your head."

The oldest son climbed down out of the tree and found a big wooden chest full of money and jewels. Next morning he set out again, this time with the box. Before long he came to a village, and he decided to settle there. He built a big new house, married one of the girls of the village, and lived happily there.

The second son walked straight ahead along the middle path, thinking sorrowfully of his father and mother. As night

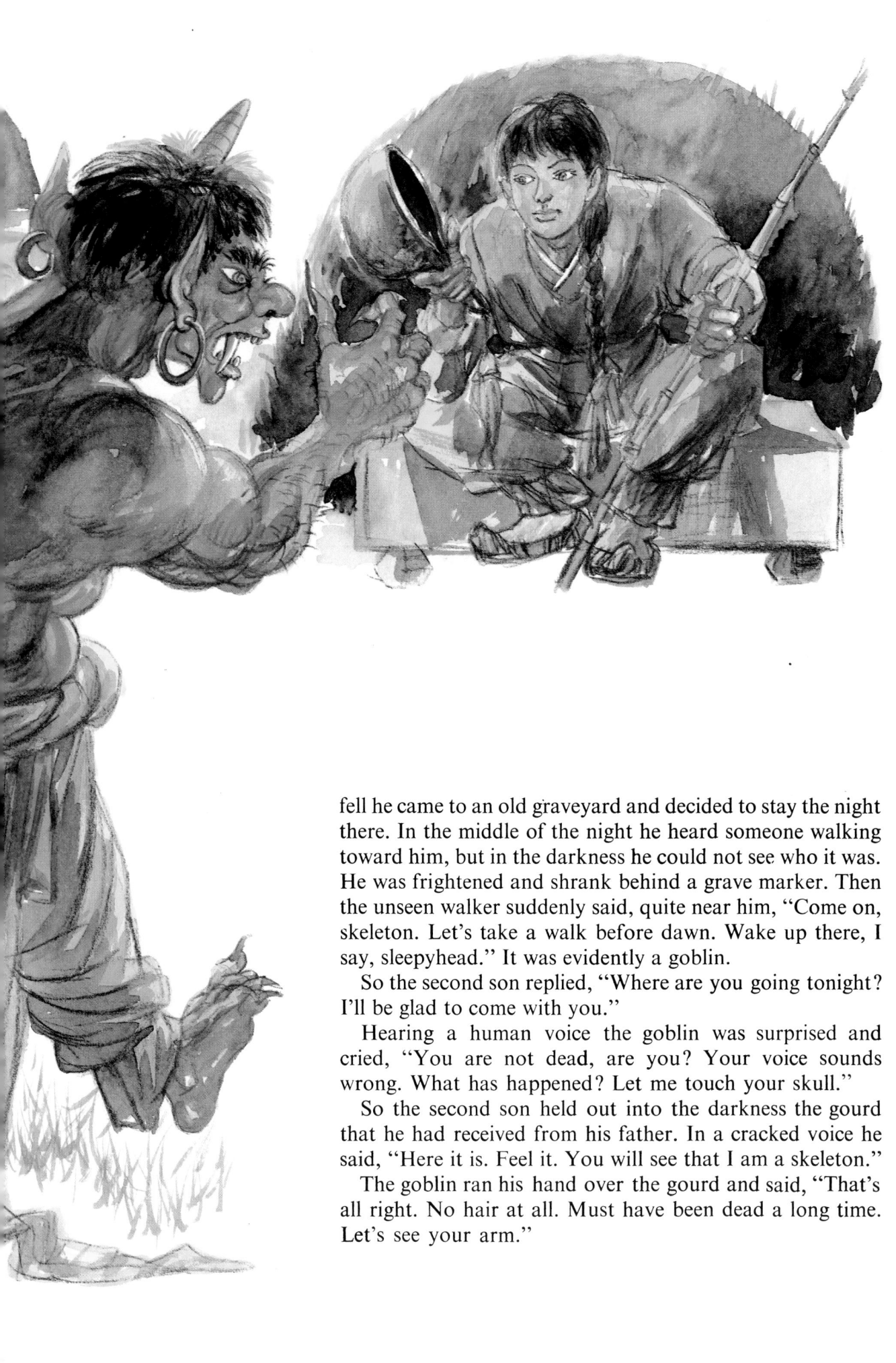

fell he came to an old graveyard and decided to stay the night there. In the middle of the night he heard someone walking toward him, but in the darkness he could not see who it was. He was frightened and shrank behind a grave marker. Then the unseen walker suddenly said, quite near him, "Come on, skeleton. Let's take a walk before dawn. Wake up there, I say, sleepyhead." It was evidently a goblin.

So the second son replied, "Where are you going tonight? I'll be glad to come with you."

Hearing a human voice the goblin was surprised and cried, "You are not dead, are you? Your voice sounds wrong. What has happened? Let me touch your skull."

So the second son held out into the darkness the gourd that he had received from his father. In a cracked voice he said, "Here it is. Feel it. You will see that I am a skeleton."

The goblin ran his hand over the gourd and said, "That's all right. No hair at all. Must have been dead a long time. Let's see your arm."

The second son held out the bamboo stick and said, "Here it is. You are hard to please, aren't you?"

The goblin felt the stick and said, "Ah, very thin indeed. You must have starved to death. Very well, let us go. Tonight we are going to steal the soul of a rich man's only daughter. Ha! Ha! Ha!"

They hurried to a village and stopped outside the gate of a large house. The goblin said, "You wait outside here, skeleton. I'll go and get the daughter's soul while she's asleep." Then he went into the house.

So the second son waited outside the house and in a few minutes the goblin came back, apparently holding something in his hand. "This is her soul," he said. "It is a very nice one indeed, you know. By the way, have you a purse or something?"

"Oh yes, I have," answered the second son. "I'll put the soul in it so that it can't escape."

He took the daughter's soul very carefully and put it in his purse. Then he drew the strings tight and went back toward the graveyard with the goblin. Before long they heard a cock crow, and the goblin said, "It is time for me to leave you. I'll meet you again soon. You had better keep the soul for the time being."

The goblin vanished, and the second son waited for dawn. When it grew light he saw that his purse was swollen as if there was some living thing inside it. Then at sunrise he went back to the village and heard that the only daughter of a rich man had died suddenly in the night, leaving her parents overcome with grief. They called in all the doctors, but to no avail, for they could not even establish the cause of death. The second son hid the purse in his shirt and went to the dead girl's father. He kept his secret to himself and said, "I think I may be able to bring your daughter back to life. Will you let me try?"

"You may if you like, stranger," replied the bereaved father. "If you can restore her to me you will earn my undying gratitude."

"Let me see her then, and let no one else as much as peep into the room while I am at work. If you will accept these conditions I will start at once."

The father accepted his offer and took him to the room where his daughter lay. The second son locked the door securely on the inside and covered the windows. He put a screen around the bed, and going behind it he held his purse right under the dead girl's nose. Then he loosened the strings and her soul flew out of the purse and into her nostrils

with a whistling sound. She opened her eyes at once and was completely restored. He unlocked the door, and the girl's parents came in. They embraced her and wept with joy. In his gratitude her father offered the second son his daughter's hand in marriage, and the boy accepted. So they were married, and the second son lived happily as the son-in-law of a wealthy family.

The youngest son set out along the road to the left. As he walked along through the mountains he amused himself by beating with his hand on the long drum which he carried slung from his neck. The mountains rang with the rhythm of the drum and the melody of his voice raised in song. Before long he saw a big yellow tiger come out of the forest and dance to his music. He was terrified at its appearance and realized that he could not stop playing, for if he did the tiger would assuredly fall upon him and eat him up. So he went on playing to keep it in good humor, and walked backward so that he could face the tiger and watch what it might do.

Before long he came to a village. All the villagers were very amused to see him, with the tiger dancing before him. It seemed to be quite tame, for it attacked no one, and people began to throw money to the youngest son. He was surprised and pleased to find he was such a success, so he led the tiger up to the capital, beating his drum and making the tiger dance.

The King was greatly interested by what he heard of this unusual happening and summoned the youngest son to come and perform at the palace. One of the King's daughters fell in love with him, and the King consented to their marriage. And so the youngest son became the husband of a royal princess, and the tiger was made a royal pet.

When ten years had gone by the three brothers, to whom their father's tokens had brought such good fortune, went back to the place where they had parted. There they told one another of the adventures which had befallen them and went together to visit the graves of their parents.

The Vanity of the Rat

Once upon a time Mr. and Mrs. Rat were anxious to marry their darling, darling daughter into a very respectable family. From the first they thought Mr. Sun to be the most high stationed and well-descended bachelor and accordingly their first choice fell on him. Mr. Rat made overtures to Mr. Sun, who, smiling gracefully, replied:

"My friend, I should rather like to recommend to you Mr. Cloud, who can stop me from shining."

This was enough to turn Mr. Rat's head toward Mr. Cloud, who waved his hand and said:

"My friend, you seem not to know that there is one who is more worthy of your honor than I. Though I often get the better of Mr. Sun, I am still a mere slave of Mr. Wind. His blast and grumble make me go where I do not want to go."

So Mr. Rat talked with Mr. Wind. Mr. Wind in turn refused to be the son-in-law of Mr. Rat and said:

"I am indeed powerful enough because forests tremble and ships toss in fear of me. But there is one who is more powerful than I. He is Mr. Statue. He sets his strong legs firmly upon the earth and stands immobile in my way, arms folded, eyes unblinking." So saying he whizzed on.

Mr. Rat wondered how his wise brain could ever have overlooked so powerful, and close a neighbor, and he visited Mr. Statue at once.

"My Friend," said Mr. Statue. "It is quite true that I can check the progress of Mr. Wind who commands Mr. Cloud who overpowers Mr. Sun. But what am I to you, 0 Mighty Mr. Rat! Your great race can undermine me and make me fall in the twinkling of an eye if need be. Mr. Rat, I am at your mercy!"

On hearing this, Mr. Rat cocked his head, his small eyes sparkling, and as if regretting his rash advances to an unworthy underling, quickly turned and made his way to his hole, all the way jabbering:

"Shame on me! Shame on me! Now I know this glorious race is next to none. Yes, next to none in respectability!"

Thus Mr. and Mrs. Rat came to content themselves with giving away their darling, darling daughter to one of their kinsmen.

The Hare's Liver

One evening, the Dragon King in his beautiful palace at the bottom of the sea complained of an acute pain in his stomach. He rolled on his coral bed, surrounded by his Queen, Princes, and Princesses, who knit their brows in deep grief. All night long he groaned continually, and the sea churned with his resounding roars. Before dawn of the next morning, he called his Cabinet Ministers into his presence and bellowed:

"I am seriously ill, and perhaps I will have to throw away my spoon (die). Last night, I tried all the medicines in my Kingdom, but to no avail. Now who can cure my singular malady?"

The cuttlefish, who was the chief physician of the court, made a low bow and, after feeling the pulse of the Dragon King, spoke: "Your Majesty will be cured immediately if you will only eat the boiled liver of a hare. Long live the King!"

"Boiled liver of a hare!" exclaimed the Dragon King. "Well, who will fetch me the hare that I may have her liver plucked out and boiled for my medicine?"

"I will strike the hare with the long sword on my nose," said the swordfish, "and I will carry her between my sharp teeth as far as Your Majesty's palace."

"No!" roared the Dragon King. "She must be brought in alive."

"I will clasp the hare with my long arms," said the octopus, "and I will present her fresh and pretty before your throne."

"No!" roared the Dragon again. "Your hard grip on her slender body will surely melt her timid liver."

There was a heavy silence. At last, the turtle prostrated himself before the Dragon King, struck his head on the floor three times, and then said, "Through my amphibious abilities, I will carry the hare on my back and bring her safely to Your Majesty."

"Good!" bellowed the Dragon King with a beam of delight. "I remember that your grandfather, in his youth, ran a marathon race with a hare, and victory went to his side. Of course, you can travel both on land and sea. Go and bring me the hare. I shall neither eat nor sleep till I have eaten the hare's liver. And in order to make your adventure more successful, I will give you a life-like portrait of the hare so that you will not make a mistake and bring back the wrong animal."

The Dragon King ordered the court artists to draw a portrait of the hare, and they immediately began drawing. One drew her eyes seeing all the beauties of nature, one drew her ears hearing the songs of cuckoos and parrots, one drew

her mouth eating orchids and fragrant herbs, one drew her snow-white fleece shielding the wintry blast, and one drew her legs bouncing in the clouds that hung over high hills and deep valleys. Thus they finished the portrait, which looked exactly like a living hare with two eyes pink and round, forelegs short and hind legs long, and two ears perked up into the air.

The turtle took leave of the Dragon King and darted up to the surface of the blue sea, and let himself drift aimlessly on the waves. After a long trip, he was glad to lumber ashore and continued his journey toward a beautiful mountain along a melodious stream.

It was spring, and all the plants and moving creatures looked happy and gay. The azaleas were breathing out a sweet perfume, the butterflies were flirting from flower to flower, the willow branches were swinging over the sapphire pools, the golden orioles were calling their mates, the homesick nightingales were singing a heart-rending song, and the swallows were twittering by way of announcing their return from the warm south, while cuckoos and thousands of other birds were warbling in their sweetest voices. All the hills and dales were shining with pink flowers and silvery streams.

Enjoying this picturesque scenery, the turtle continued up the hill looking for traces of the hare.

After a while, he saw a crowd of wild animals run downhill—squirrels, deer, wolves, bears, wild boars, tigers, panthers, weasels, monkeys, elephants, foxes, etc. . . but no hare was to be seen.

The turtle stretched his neck and looked all around, and at last, his eyes found a pretty creature which resembled the portrait he had brought. He looked at this creature and then at the portrait, and he was sure that this was the animal he wanted. He was exceedingly glad at heart and, for some time, he watched the movements of the hare, who nibbled at fresh grass and vines, and leaped on the hanging rocks as she danced round and round.

The turtle finally cleared his throat and addressed her in a flattering speech: "Good morning, Miss Hare! I have heard so much of your fragrant name, and wanted to see you once in my life. How happy I am to meet you here today in this beautiful spring!"

Hereupon, the hare replied: "I have traveled all over the earth and come across so many living things, but I have never seen such an ugly creature as you. Your toeless feet, your neck playing hide-and-seek, and your back, rugged and round—these are all very funny. At first glimpse, you look like a wooden bowl. Who in the world are you?"

The turtle, of course, was much displeased upon hearing the abusive words, but the controlled his temper and answered: "My name is Turtle but I am better known as the 'Byuljooboo.' My back is round so I never sink when floating on the waves; my neck is long so I can see far and wide; my body is round so I can behave myself as an all-round perfect gentleman. Therefore, I am the hero of the water and the captain of all sea creatures. I can proudly say that I am unexcelled in both civil and military arts on land and sea.

"Miss Hare! You are very proud of your wide travels on land. But have you seen the bottom of the sea with its wonderful gardens, wonderful plants, and wonderful fish around the water palace of the Dragon King? No painter can capture the submarine beauty. If you ride on my back, I will show you all these wonders, and the Dragon King will treat you like a princess. You will eat all kinds of delicious seafood and dance with the handsome princes in the palace.''

The hare was seized with a strong curiosity to see the splendors of the water palace, so she immediately jumped upon the back of the turtle, who, after a long and deep dive, brought her to the water palace under the South Sea.

While the hare was sitting in an ante-chamber adjoining the audience hall, ready to be received by the Dragon King, an army of rude soldiers rushed in, bound her hands and feet as they cried, "King's Order! King's Order!" and took her before the dragon throne without ceremony.

The hare trembled from head to foot, for her astonishment was beyond description. When she looked up, her large pink eyes met a monstrous giant with a multi-horned coral crown glittering on his head, a long silvery robe of reversed fins shining over his carp-like body, two fiery eyes flashing on his brow, and a pearl scepter sparkling in his hand. He was sitting on his throne, surrounded by hundreds of civilian and military officers. His huge mouth, with spear-like teeth, was grinning, and a long crimson tongue lolled down, seemingly ready to swallow the hare in one mouthful at any moment. This was the Dragon King, for the hare's quivering ears heard a thundering voice ringing out of his mouth. His royal message was repeated by a herald:

"Listen, you hare! The face, the robe, and the throne of a king or an emperor is called the dragon face, the dragon robe, and the dragon throne after My Majesty. I am the great

King of the Sea, and you are only a small creature of the hill. I am suffering from an unusual malady, and nothing but your liver will cure my disease. So I sent the turtle and brought you here. You are expected not to regret your death. When you are dead, my servants will shroud your body with fine silk and embroidered brocade, and put it into a casket of pearl and amber. Your burial ground shall be in a beautiful garden behind my palace. Moreover, when your liver cures my disease and restores my perpetual youth, I will have a shrine erected with a pretty monument to the memory of your extraordinary merit. You are more fortunate to die a noble death than to become the prey of a tiger or the game of a hunter on the hill. I promise you all these high honors which are reserved for a princess of the blood. You have every reason to be thankful instead of resentful. Now get ready to die with a happy look."

Then, rolling his eyes to left and right, the Dragon King commanded his servants to split the belly of the hare and take out her liver. All at once, the ferocious soldiers, who stood in the courtyard, rushed forward as they brandished their lightning swords, which they readied to plunge into her belly.

It was a shocking bolt from the blue, and the poor little hare would have fainted away had she not had great presence of mind. She summoned her courage and wit, and spoke to the Dragon King in a clarion voice:

"Your Majesty! Permit me to make a farewell address before my death. A humble creature like myself would gladly embrace death if it could restore the health of a noble king. Rather, I am grateful for your royal bounty in preparing my splendid funeral with such great ceremony. But I regret to say that, unlike other creatures, my mother fell in love with a star in the Milky Way and conceived me of the celestial spirit. From the moment of my birth, I sipped the morning dew and ate fragrant grass together with medicinal herbs. By and by, my liver became a wonderful remedy that could cure all, plus give perpetual youth to he who partakes of it. So all people on land begged me to give them my liver to eat. In order to get rid of this constant begging, I plucked out my liver together with my heart with mine own hands, washed them many times in a clean mountain stream, and hid them in a secret place on the hill. All unexpectedly, I met the turtle and traveled on his back to your palace. Had I known your singular malady, I would have brought my liver with me . . . ."

The Dragon King, hearing this story and seeing the composed air of the hare, wondered whether her words were not true. He roared at the hare:

"How can you pull out your liver and push it back so easily?"

The hare was almost sure of her escape now and answered: "The Heaven was opened in the hour of the rat, the earth was formed in the hour of the cow, the first man was born in the hour of the tiger, and all creatures came out in the hour of the hare. Therefore, I am above ten thousand birds and animals. Even the benevolent giraffe and the noble phoenix bow and sing of my creative work. Can I not play at such easy magic as removing and replacing the liver in my own body?"

The Dragon King was a very generous sovereign by nature. He remained silent for a while as he told himself, "If I cannot get her liver after ripping her belly open, I shall have killed a fair creature in vain, and there would be no one to give me the wonderful liver. Judging from her earnest voice and bold looks, I believe that the hare is not telling a lie. I had better send her home to bring back her liver." So he gave two hundred sparkling pearls to the hare and spoke in a mild voice:

"Take this small present as a souvenir of your first visit to my water palace. Go in peace and come back soon with your liver."

The hare took the royal gift with a bow and, mounting on the back of the turtle, she started on her homeward voyage.

After rolling merrily on the blue waves, the turtle tossed his fair rider upon the shore.

The hare could not help rejoicing in her escape from a watery grave and the stomach of the Dragon King. So she danced round and round in all directions. Seeing this, the turtle ordered the hare to pick up her liver and return to the water palace immediately.

The hare laughed heartily till her sides almost split and she really tossed out her liver.

"What a turtle you are!" she cried. "Now I can understand the phrase 'as foolish as a turtle.' Do you still believe that I can pull out and push back my liver like a toy? I fooled your Dragon King and his whole court. After all, the malady of your Dragon King has nothing to do with me. You kidnaped me with a fine trick in order to live yourself more happily at the cost of my life. So I feel very much like killing you, but, considering your good service in carrying me to and from the water palace through winds and waves, I pardon your crime and spare your remaining life. Now you go back and tell your Dragon King to forget my liver, and kiss death with a glad heart, for no medicine can guarantee immortal life or constantly keep away death, which embraces a prince or a peasant as equals when the zero hour comes."

The hare laughed again, and, clutching the pearls, trotted into the forest, to be seen no more.

Kongji and Patji

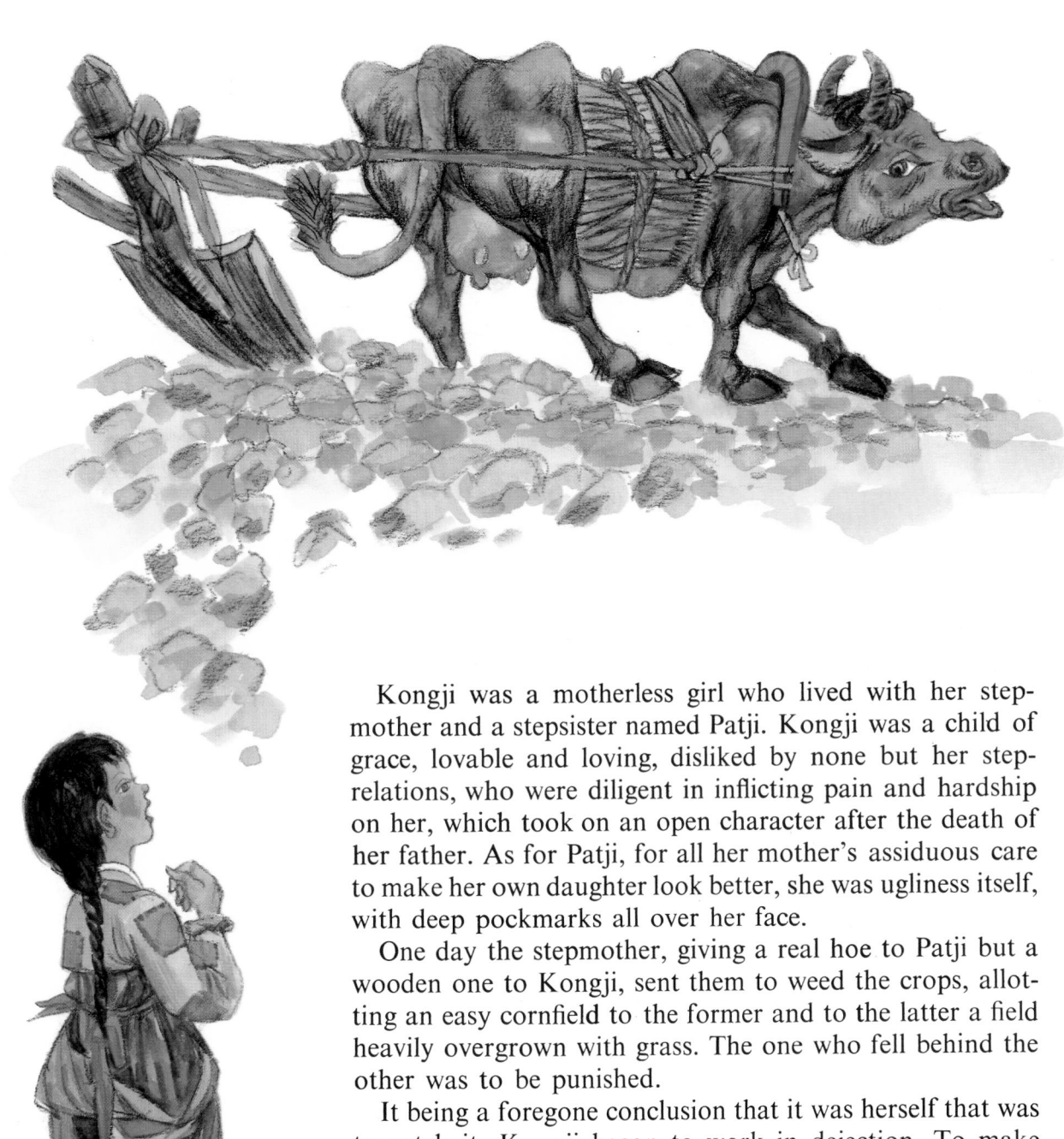

Kongji was a motherless girl who lived with her stepmother and a stepsister named Patji. Kongji was a child of grace, lovable and loving, disliked by none but her steprelations, who were diligent in inflicting pain and hardship on her, which took on an open character after the death of her father. As for Patji, for all her mother's assiduous care to make her own daughter look better, she was ugliness itself, with deep pockmarks all over her face.

One day the stepmother, giving a real hoe to Patji but a wooden one to Kongji, sent them to weed the crops, allotting an easy cornfield to the former and to the latter a field heavily overgrown with grass. The one who fell behind the other was to be punished.

It being a foregone conclusion that it was herself that was to catch it, Kongji began to work in dejection. To make matters worse, her hoe caught in the hard ground and broke. She burst into violent sobbing. The suppressed grief from a long series of wrongs suffered at the hands of her steprelations made her cry beyond control. She wished loudly that her dead mother might take her to herself or, if she was unworthy of such a kindness, that a tiger might put an end to her miserable life.

All of a sudden she felt a strange presence and, lifting her eyes, beheld a black cow with soothing, understanding eyes. The very sight of the cow put heart into her. Without knowing why she was filled with wonder and gladness. When the

cow heard the reason of her weeping, it offered to help.
Kongji believed the cow to be the shadow of her own mother.
The quick movements with which the black cow used its
feet, horns and even its teeth was marvellous, and soon the
work was finished.

It was not enough for the spiteful step-relations to deny the
poor friendless child the pleasures they themselves enjoyed;
they used to set her to extra tasks that were sometimes
impossible to perform. Once, when the stepmother took her
own daughter to a birthday party, to which they had been
invited, she ordered Kongji to fill a jar and a caldron —
both of which had cracked bottoms — with water. Of
course, failure to do so meant severe punishment.

After trying without success for hours to fill the containers,
she broke down with a sob. Suddenly two toads of tremen-
dous size appeared and each crept into one of the leaking
vessels. Heartened by the appearance of the toads, she
again started filling the vessels, and this time was successful.
When the family came back, perhaps looking forward to
torturing Kongji for not filling the vessels, they were
astounded to find the miracle performed. Concealing her
amazement, however, the stepmother remarked that even
Kongji, the fool of a girl, could do something once in a while.

Another time, Patji and her mother were going out to a
wedding party held some distance away. Dressed in their
best gowns and wearing trinkets and riding in a covered

sedan, they set out, leaving Kongji to another heart-breaking task—drying and husking a huge mound of rice, a week's work for any one person. In order to have a clean conscience, they added that she could come too, when the work was done.

Scarcely had the crestfallen child spread the grain on a number of straw mats to dry, when a vast flock of sparrows alighted and covered the length and breadth of the spread grain. So afraid was she that the birds might consume the rice in a minute, she shouted at them frantically to scare them away. But they would not be scared away.

There was nothing she could do but resign herself to her fate when she noticed, to her increasing surprise, that the sparrows did not so much as touch a single grain; that

instead they were only husking with their sharp beaks while flapping their wings all the time to dry the grain. Thus the work was soon completed, and all that remained to be done was to gather the prepared grain into straw bags.

The task now finished, the yearning to go and see the wedding grew stronger in Kongji. But how was she to get fine clothes to wear? Who was there to provide her with a respectable sedan and its bearers? And the money to tip the servants with? While she was thus lost in her thoughts, the black cow again suddenly appeared as if it had just popped up out of the ground right in front of the dreaming child. "Hold your hands closely by my side, child," said the cow, "and you shall have whatever you wish for, as I carry everything in my sides."

As from a magic wand, there streamed out of the black cow beautiful clothes, shoes, ornaments of gold and silver and what not, in short, enough to make an ugly woman fair and a fair woman bewitching. Then came a delightfully decorated sedan born by four bearers. Even the two graceful handmaids were not forgotten. Everything was as spick and span as would have befitted a princess.

A hush fell upon the wedding party when the brilliant procession was sighted a hundred paces off. "What lady of station can it be?" was the query on every lip. Even Kongji's stepmother was forced to hold her tongue; she dared not acknowledge the beautiful maiden as her downtrodden stepdaughter.

Everyone was overpowered by Kongji's beauty, and as luck would have it the Governor was attending the party, and more than anyone else he was so struck by her beauty that he insisted that he had to have her for his wife.

Kongji was at first reluctant to accept for she was uneducated and unfit to be the wife of such a noble man. The Governor questioned her closely on her background, and was all the more impressed by her modesty and sincerity. He said that she was the only woman who could make him happy and without her he would surely die a lonesome old man.

Thus Kongji accepted and moved into his residence with all its fine trimmings, gold in-laid chests and soft silks.

The stepmother and Patji became very jealous of Kongji's good fortune and together worked out a wicked plan to ruin her and get the Governor's fortune for themselves.

And so it was one day that Patji called upon Kongji apologizing for the sins she and her stepmother had committed against Kongji in the past and begging Kongji's forgiveness. Kongji was so kind-hearted that she readily forgave, and to show that there were no ill feelings she prepared a wonderful meal for Patji and happily showed her the glittering furniture and cabinets filled with many dozens of dresses in silk and brocade. Then she took Patji out to the garden to show her the lotus pond her husband so admired.

Patji, seeing her chance, begged permission to take a bath in the pond and saying she did not like to bath alone persuaded Kongji to enter the pond also. After swimming to the middle of the pond, Patji quickly rose up and forced Kongji to the bottom, from whence a few bubbles rose to the surface, the only sign of something amiss. Patji returned to shore and with very heavy makeup and Kongji's clothes managed to pass herself off to the Governor as his wife. But she could only manage to do this by telling the Governor that she was terribly ill and must remain in bed for a very long period of time to recover. The Governor thought this was very strange as Kongji had always been so healthy and full of laughter, but as he loved her so much and wanted only the best for her, he told all the attendants his wife must have complete rest and ordered them to fill her every wish.

One evening the Governor went to his favorite spot by the lotus pond to breath the evening air, and he noticed a large

lotus flower that seemed to nod to him. Its beauty so reminded him of his beautiful wife before she took ill, that he decided she must have it, and he plucked it out of the pond and ordered that it be put in a vase and placed by his wife's bed.

Patji awoke in the morning and after seeing the flower and learning from whence it came, saw in it only the ghost of Kongji. She ordered that the flower be taken from her room and thrown in the fireplace in the kitchen and destroyed.

The following morning, an old woman living nearby came into the kitchen to get some live coals for her fire as, being a good friend of the Governor's wife, she had done so many times in the past. But, instead of live coals, she found many beads rolling around and, being fond of beads and thinking these were thrown away, she picked them up and later put them in a corner of her cabinet. Soon, from inside the cabinet, she heard someone calling her name.

The old woman was startled; she opened her cabinet and found Kongji sitting there. Kongji then told her the whole story about her wicked step-relations and how Patji had

drowned her in the lotus pond. Kongji asked for her help to win her husband back, and the two quickly worked out a plan.

The next day the old woman prepared her best food and spread a large table. She then went to the Governor's house and saying that it was her birthday she wanted to share her evening meal with someone and since the Governor's wife was ill and he was forced to eat alone, the old woman would be honored to invite him to her home, though she was unworthy to do so. The Governor laughed and was soon sitting at the table, filled with sumptuous food.

"You are an excellent cook," said the Governor, "and your food draws my good appetite." So saying he took hold of his chopsticks but, to his great annoyance, he discovered that one was longer than the other and he could not pick up any food. "Look here, old woman," he said. "These chopsticks are not paired to each other. Why do you treat me in such a fashion?"

But before the old woman could open her mouth to reply a voice came from behind a screen: "Aaaah, you are clever enough to detect an unmatched pair of chopsticks, but not clever enough to detect a mismatched man and wife."

The voice was so much like his wife's before she became ill, that he was forced to think of the strange happenings around his house of late. The Governor remembered that everything had been wonderful until the evening he found his wife by the lotus pond when she told him she was very ill. Then he remembered the nodding lotus flower!

Immediately upon returning home he ordered the lotus pond be drained of water whereupon Kongji was discovered at the bottom on a bed of lotus flowers and leaves. Her face was turned upward and she was still as beautiful as ever.

The Governor quickly sent for the fake wife and ordered her from his house and told her that neither her nor her mother were ever to set foot in the village again.

The town's people set about preparing a funeral for Kongji. Her body was brought before the Governor and, after services, she was about to be lowered into a casket bedecked with lotus flowers, when all at once, the dead beauty drew a deep breath and came back to life.

The Governor apologized to Kongji for his blindness in the past and rewarded the old woman living next door. He lived very happy with Kongji, who brought forth three sons and two daughters.

The fame of Kongji, like the fragrance of the lotus, spread far and wide, and her womanly virtue is remembered to this day.

The Ant That Laughed Too Much

Little Ok Cha and her grandmother were laughing. All
the other people around, grownups and children alike, were

laughing, too. Their olive-skinned faces were crinkled with smiles, and their narrow, almond-shaped eyes twinkled with fun. The inner court rang with the sound of their merriment.

The cause of it all was Ok Cha's brother, Yong Tu. He was trying to stand on his head as he had seen the funny acrobats do at the fair in the city the day before. It had been a splendid fair, with clowns and tightrope walkers and tumblers who could do many more tricks than turning themselves upside down. Yong Tu could imitate the antics of the clowns, but he had nothing on which to try the tightrope walking. It was perhaps a good thing, for he was having enough difficulty on the ground, pretending to be a traveling tumbler.

The boy's long braid of black hair kept getting in his way, until his grandmother loaned him a hairpin to fasten the braid up on the crown of his head. This made Ok Cha laugh louder than ever. She laughed and laughed, until her very sides ached.

"Take care, child," her grandmother warned her. "Take care, or like the ant that laughed too much, you will meet with disaster."

"What happened to the ant, Grandma?" the little girl asked, with one eye still on Yong Tu. He had tired of trying to get his feet up into the air and was now rolling about on the ground, playing with their dog which everyone simply called "Dog."

"You shall hear, blessed girl," the old grandmother said, hoping to calm the giggling child.

"This ant was a wise old ant and greatly respected in the garden where she lived. Everyone came to her for advice, and so it was not at all strange that the earthworm should choose her to act as a go-between and find him a wife.

" 'I badly want a good wife, ant,' the earthworm said, 'someone who will take care of my clothes and prepare my meals. Find me a young wife, a healthy and strong one. I know you will choose wisely.'

"The ant agreed. She was thinking over the problem one sunny afternoon, when she met a strong, healthy centipede.

" 'How would you like to become a bride?' the ant asked the young centipede.

" 'Well enough! Well enough!' was the centipede's reply. 'But you must tell me first about the bridegroom.'

" 'The bridegroom is industrious. He is calm and he is patient,' the ant replied with enthusiasm.

" 'Does he live in this garden?' the centipede asked.

" 'Yes, he lives in this garden, though often he is out of sight of those who walk on its paths.'

" 'That is true of all garden creatures,' the centipede said. 'Tell me more about the bridegroom.'

" 'Well, he is many times longer than you, and he moves about well, although he has no legs.'

" 'That would be a fine centipede,' the prospective bride said with scorn. 'What kind of husband for me would be one without any legs?'

" 'He is an honorable earthworm,' the ant then confessed.

" 'Ugh! A damp, clammy earthworm!' The centipede shook her head. 'An earthworm would never do. His body is way too long. I would never have patience enough to make a coat for such a long creature.'

"The ant thought this very funny. She laughed and she laughed as she scurried down the garden path to tell the bad news to the waiting bridegroom.

" 'Oh, earthworm,' she said between her fits of laughter. 'I found a young bride, a beautiful centipede, healthy and strong, but she will have none of you. She says she will never have a husband without any legs. She says you are too long. She would never have patience enough to make your clothes.' And the ant went off into fits of laughter again.

" 'I do not find this joke funny,' the earthworm said indignantly. 'Why should a centipede laugh at a fine earthworm like me? I will not have her either. With all those legs of hers! No! A thousand times, no! How would I ever get enough straw to make shoes for so many feet? Forget the whole idea.'

"Well, the ant thought this even funnier than the remarks of the centipede. She laughed and she laughed until her sides ached. She feared she would burst. So she took a straw rope and tied herself tightly about the middle.

"Only when she had forgotten about her adventures as go-between for the earthworm and the centipede, did the ant untie the rope. And what do you think had happened, Ok Cha?" The grandmother paused for a moment, enjoying the little girl's eager, questioning face.

"That ant had laughed too much. Her waist was so firmly pinched in by the straw rope that it never grew large again. Remember this story, Ok Cha, the next time you meet an ant on the path in our garden. Then you will understand why the ant's waist is so small."